endangered plants

Dorothy Childs Hogner

endangered plants

Illustrated by
Arabelle Wheatley

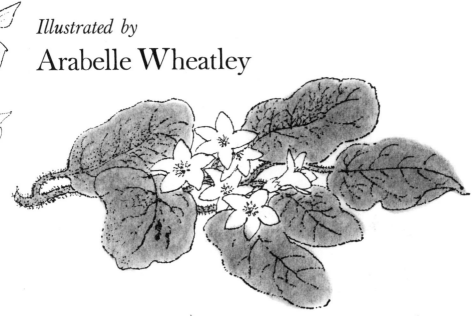

Thomas Y. Crowell Company   *New York*

To the memory of dear Nils
and our many travels together
in America from the Gaspé Peninsula
down into Mexico

Library of Congress Cataloging in Publication Data
Hogner, Dorothy Childs. Endangered plants.
Includes index.
1. Rare plants—United States—
Juv. lit. 2. Plant conservation—United States—Juv.
lit. 3. Wild flower gardening—United States—Juvenile
literature. I. Wheatley, Arabelle. II. Title.
QK86.U6H63   581.9'73   77-2310
ISBN 0-690-01362-0
10 9 8 7 6 5 4 3 2 1

Acknowledgments

While doing research for this book, the author has called upon many experts for assistance. First and foremost she wishes to thank Dr. Robert A. DeFilipps of the Endangered Flora Project, Department of Botany, National Museum of Natural History, Smithsonian Institution, Washington, D.C., for reading the manuscript. His suggestions were very helpful.

Among other authorities who have answered her questions, the author wishes to thank the following:

George R. Stephens, Forester, The Connecticut Agricultural Experiment Station, New Haven, Connecticut; John E. Hibbard, Secretary-Forester, Connecticut Forest and Park Association, East Hartford, Connecticut; Peter A. Hyypio, Extension Botanist, Cooperative Extension, New York State, Cornell University, Ithaca, New York; James W. Hardin, Professor of Botany and Forestry, North Carolina State University, Raleigh, North Carolina; Senator Harold E. Hughes, Honorary National Chairman, and John P. Hansel, Executive Director, Elm Research Institute, Harrisville, New Hampshire; Ronald L. McGregor, Director, State Biological Survey of Kansas, University of Kansas, Lawrence, Kansas; Richard Pardo, Programs Director, American Forestry Association, Washington D.C.; Alice Q. Howard, Administrative Assistant, Herbarium, Department of Botany, University of California, Berkeley, California; Anthony Wayne Smith, President, National Parks and Conservation Association, Washington, D.C.; Virginia F. Martin, Secretary, The Cactus and Succulent Society of America, Arcadia, California.

Contents

Introduction

Endangered plants are plants that are in danger of becoming extinct. An extinct plant is gone forever. Never again will it be seen growing in the wild.

In the United States the first list made of endangered species included only wild animals, birds, reptiles and amphibians, and fishes. Plants were not on this list. By the year 1966, several birds and fishes had become extinct, gone forever from this world. In that same year, and again in 1969, Endangered Species Acts were published by the Bureau of Sport Fisheries and Wildlife of the United States Government. The endangered wildlife included the grizzly bear, the bowhead whale, the southern bald eagle, the whooping crane, the American alligator, and the Atlantic salmon.

Not until the Endangered Species Act of 1973 were plants included. In January of 1975, S. Dillon Ripley, Secretary of the Smithsonian Institution, presented to Congress the Report on Endangered and Threatened Plant Species of the United States. Only native species of the higher plants (ferns, flowers, shrubs, and trees) are included. This report was printed by the United States Government Printing Office, Washington, D.C. (see Appendix 1). As of now, the federal government lists plants that are endangered, or threatened with becoming extinct, and federal agencies are required to develop programs to conserve the officially listed plants, under the provisions of the Endangered Species Act of 1973.

The plants described in this book are among those classified by the Smithsonian report as endangered, threatened, commercially exploited, or extinct.

endangered plants

Look-See

Would you like to know the wild plants of America? The first thing to do is to look at them. Go for a walk. If you live in the country, take a walk along a roadside. Walk through a field. Go into the cow pasture. Walk along the edge of the woods. Walk through the woods. And look.

If you live in the city, walk in the park. You will find some wild plants there, too. Better still, when you go to the country for a vacation, look and see there.

And when you spot a plant that you admire, say a wild flower, do not pick it. Study it. Enjoy its beauty and go get a book on wild flowers. If you do not have a book on wild flowers on your own bookshelf, borrow one from the library. Go through the book until you find the plant you are looking for.

Lady's Slipper

Suppose that the wild flower you have found is a beautiful lady's slipper. It is called a lady's slipper because of the shape of the lip of the flower.

1

Thirty different kinds of lady's slippers are native to North America. The most common, the large, yellow lady's slipper (*Cypripedium parviflorum* var. *pubescens*) reaches a height of two feet. This lady's slipper grows in woods and woody bogs from eastern Canada and Maine south along the mountains to Alabama and west to Washington and Oregon. The one flower on each plant usually blossoms in June. Note: The hairs on leaves and stems of the yellow and some other lady's slippers give off an acid that can cause skin trouble, particularly in hot weather, or if the person who touches the plant is perspiring.

The moccasin flower (*Cypripedium acaule*) is also a rather common lady's slipper which grows in woods, on rocky ledges, and often in bogs from central and eastern Canada to Maine, south to North Carolina, Tennessee, Kentucky, Georgia, and Alabama, and west to Minnesota. The flower stalk is usually from eight to twelve inches high but sometimes reaches two feet. The one flower, deep pink in color, blooms from late May to early June. The two leaves come not from the flower stalk but from the roots.

The showy lady's slipper (*Cypripedium reginae*), with white petals and a rose pouch, is the state flower of Minnesota.

Now which lady's slipper have you found? What color is the flower? Suppose the pouch, or lip, is white outside, streaked with purple inside, and the petals are greenish. Then you have found the rare white lady's slipper (*Cypripedium candidum*) which grows in wet meadows and bogs and on the prairies in eastern Canada and fifteen states from New York, New Jersey, and Pennsylvania south to Kentucky and west to Missouri, Minnesota, and the Dakotas. It is small, at the most a foot high. There are three to five leaves on the flowering stalk, and one or two flowers on each plant. It blossoms in May and June.

The first thing that you should learn about this lady's slipper is, is it endangered? In danger of what?

white lady's slipper
(Cypripedium candidum)

Endangered Plants

You hear these two words a lot these days. If they were about a person, you might think that he or she was in danger of being held up with a gun. But what do the words mean when speaking of a plant?

A plant may be endangered in several ways. A particular plant may be endangered because it is being picked or dug up too much. Other plants may be injured by insects or disease.

A major cause of plants becoming endangered is destruction of habitat. Habitat is the word that describes the place where a plant grows. It is a wild plant's home: a field, a pasture, a roadside, a forest, a brookside, or, if it is a water plant, a river, pond, lake, or the seashore.

In a field, suppose someone comes along on a snowmobile. He plows a path down to the ground, destroying the plants growing there. A man with a bulldozer can be much more destructive. He tears up the soil and kills all of the wild plants. He swooshes them away.

Everywhere carpenters build dozens and hundreds and thousands of houses and stores and factories. People build towns and they build cities. More and more of the land where wild plants used to grow in America is being taken over for construction.

An example of a plant endangered by construction is the Tennessee cone flower (*Echinacea tennesseensis*). This pretty

4

Tennessee
cone flower
(Echinacea
tennesseensis)

plant with purple-colored flowers grows up to five feet high. It is found on cedar barrens.

What about our white lady's slipper? Is it in danger of becoming extinct?

First, just what are extinct plants?

Extinct Plants

Extinct plants are plants that are gone forever from the places in the country where they used to grow. You can look for a certain plant from New York to California and not find a single one of its kind in the wild. There are now about one hundred species of extinct plants that used to grow wild on the United States mainland.

You may see a few of them in a botanical garden. But there are none growing wild out in the field, in the desert, along a roadside, or in the woods where they used to live.

To return to our white lady's slipper, you saw one growing in the wild. So, you know that it is not extinct. But is it endangered?

How You Find Out Which Plants Are Endangered

Ask your teacher or librarian to let you look at the national list of endangered plants for the United States, prepared by the Smithsonian Institution in Washington, D.C., with the help of botanists from all across the country (see Appendix 1). This report lists 761 kinds of higher plants in danger in the continental United States.

The higher plants are ferns, flowers, shrubs, and trees.

But do not try to look for the name "white lady's slipper" on *this* list. You must use the botanical name. Only botanical names are listed. About thirty states have produced individual state lists which often include common names.

The lady's slippers belong to the orchid family (Orchidaceae). We have already listed the botanical names of the lady's slippers that we have described. So, is *Cypripedium candidum* (the white lady's slipper) on the endangered plant list? No, it is not.

But there is a second list, just as important. It is the list of threatened plants.

Threatened Plants

What are threatened plants? Threatened plants are plants that could soon be on the endangered list. That is, if many more of them are picked, or dug up, or their habitats destroyed, they will become endangered. There are now 1,238 kinds of native wild plants threatened in the continental United States, according to the Smithsonian report.

Is our white lady's slipper, the *Cypripedium candidum*, on this list of threatened plants? *Yes*, in the states of Kentucky, Missouri, New Jersey, New York, North Dakota, and Pennsylvania.

There are two other lady's slippers on this list: the ram's head and the California lady's slipper.

The small ram's head lady's slipper (*Cypripedium arietinum*) grows only about six inches high. It is called the ram's head because of the shape of its one flower, which is red and white in color. It is found in bogs and wet woods in nine states from Maine to New York, west to Michigan, Wisconsin, and Minnesota, and northward into Canada. It blooms in May. It is on the Smithsonian threatened list in Vermont, Massachusetts, New York, Michigan, Wisconsin, Minnesota, and three other states.

The California lady's slipper (*Cypripedium californicum*) grows on wet hillsides and rocky ledges in evergreen forests in California and Oregon. It is on the Smithsonian threatened list in both these states. The California lady's slipper sometimes reaches over two feet in height. It has six to twelve yellowish-green flowers, spaced an inch or so apart on the stem.

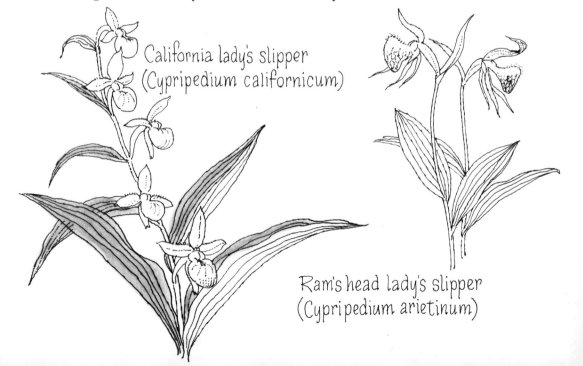

California lady's slipper
(Cypripedium californicum)

Ram's head lady's slipper
(Cypripedium arietinum)

Now, you ask, what can I do to help save these beautiful lady's slippers?

First do not pick or dig them or any other lady's slippers, even if they are not now in danger or threatened. Leave them all growing where they do best, in the wild.

Second, if you find a threatened lady's slipper, or any other threatened or endangered plant, report its location to your local plant society or the department of botany at the nearest state university or state department of conservation. If the area is on public land, you might work with the help of a Girl or Boy Scout or 4-H Club leader, to map the area and mark it for protection.

Third, make a poster. When you find an endangered or threatened plant, such as the white lady's slipper, make a picture of it. If you are an artist, by all means do a drawing or a painting. If not, get your camera. If you do not have a camera, ask a friend who has one to come along with you. Then, snap a picture.

When you have the drawing or painting finished, or the camera film developed, mount the picture on a piece of cardboard. Then, in big, bold letters, print the common name of the plant underneath the picture. In this case, "white lady's slipper." Underneath that write, "DO NOT PICK, DO NOT DIG UP THIS PLANT."

Print your name at the bottom of the cardboard.

Ask your teacher to let you put this poster up on the bulletin board at school. Or, if it is vacation time, ask for permission to put the poster in the library, town hall, grocery store, or other public place in your town.

When people see your name on the poster and ask you why they should not pick or dig up this lady's slipper, tell them: "This plant is rare. We want to save it from being picked and dug to death. Lady's slippers, like many other plants, are difficult to transplant. They grow best where they grow naturally, in their wild habitat."

Your poster may help save the white lady's slipper from dying out in your area.

Why Do We Need Plants?

As everyone knows, we need many kinds of plants for our food: vegetables like carrots, potatoes, and lettuce and grains like wheat, rye, and oats, to mention a few. We need plants to feed the animals on the farm: pasture grasses, hay, and grains for beef cattle, milk cows, and horses, and for sheep, from which we get both meat and wool. And we need grain also to feed the chickens from which we get eggs and meat.

We need trees for making lumber and paper and for fuel.

We also need certain plants for medicine. One of the most famous plants used for medicine is a tree that grows in the Andes Mountains of South America, the cinchona tree. Quinine, the medicine used to cure malaria, is made from the bark of the cinchona tree.

We need fiber plants, such as cotton, to make cloth, and hemp to make rope.

We need some plants, and the bark of certain trees, to make dyes.

But, you ask, what has this to do with other plants, with plants we do not use? The answer is that we never know when we may have to replace one of our useful plants. For instance, some day we may run out of good cereal plants. We may then need to grow a new type of plant by crossing the tired old plants with rare wild grain species.

And we never know when we may find another wild plant or shrub or tree, perhaps a rare, endangered species now growing in the wild, which will become useful in our lives. Besides that, there is always the thought of preserving wild plants, both rare and common, so that we may enjoy their beauty.

Who Are the Plant Pickers and Diggers?

They are the people who go out and pick rare wild plants, such as the lady's slippers, to put in vases in their homes. They are the people who dig up rare plants to put in their gardens, or in pots on their porches. They are the people who make a business

Ladies' tresses
(Spiranthes
lanceolata
var. paludicola)

Five-leaf orchid
(Isotria medeoloides)

of collecting rare wild plants from their native habitat to sell to you and me.

There is a list of the threatened and endangered plants that are commercially exploited and privately collected in the Smithsonian report. These include cactus plants; lady's slippers and other plants of the orchid family, such as ladies' tresses and the five-leaf orchid; and American ginseng, a plant used for medicine.

12

Ladies' Tresses

The pretty ladies' tresses are a group of orchids that grow in swamps and ditches and swampy meadows from Maine south to Florida and west to the Mississippi River.

The common ladies' tresses are the last orchids to flower, and bloom from July until October. They have a cluster of yellowish to white flowers toward the top of the stem, which is from six to twenty-four inches high. The narrow leaves are not as tall as the flower stalk.

One endangered variety of ladies' tresses (*Spiranthes lanceolata* var. *paludicola*) grows in Florida. Another Florida species (*Spiranthes polyantha*) is threatened. And a species (*Spiranthes parksii*) from Texas is possibly extinct.

Five-Leaf Orchid, Small-Whorled Pogonia

This five-leaf orchid (*Isotria medeoloides*), also called the small-whorled pogonia, has five leaves at the top of the plant, just underneath the one flower. The flower has yellowish-green petals and a pale green lip, tinged with purple at the sides. This endangered orchid grows in swampy woods in thirteen states from New England to Florida and west to Illinois and Missouri. It is on the Smithsonian endangered list in Connecticut, Illinois,

Massachusetts, Michigan, Missouri, New Hampshire, New Jersey, New York, North Carolina, Pennsylvania, Rhode Island, Vermont, and Virginia.

Cactus Plants

Like corn, tomato, and tobacco, cactus plants (family Cactaceae) are native to the New World. The only cacti growing in the Old World came from North or South America. They are among the most interesting of wild plants.

The plants themselves are strange in form and the flowers are beautiful. Some cacti have fruit that is good to eat.

Most kinds of cacti grow in the hot, dry desert country. But many are also found outside of the desert. Some grow in the subtropical forests of southern Florida, and others grow in the spruce forests of the Northwest. And some type of native cactus is found in every state in the United States except Maine, New Hampshire, Vermont, Alaska, and Hawaii.

There are about 268 kinds of cactus in the United States. They are among the plants most in need of protection. Because they make such interesting potted plants, they are often dug up. People who sell cactus plants sometimes dig them up by the truckload. There are sixty-eight species on the Smithsonian endangered and threatened lists.

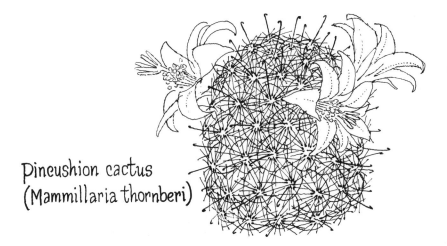

Pincushion cactus
(Mammillaria thornberi)

PINCUSHION CACTUS

Among the most common and well-known cactus plants is the pretty pincushion (genus *Mammillaria*). Pincushion cacti are sold in quantity by dealers. They are small, only a few inches high, or at most a foot. The whole plant looks like a dome. At the top of each tuber is a circle of spines. Each spine is about an inch long and has whitish hairs when the plant is young. There are no hairs on the spines of old plants.

Pincushion cacti often grow in large clumps. Hundreds of them may form one big mound.

There are two hundred different kinds of pincushion cacti in the United States, Mexico, and the West Indies.

15

The largest, the devil's pincushion, has reddish spines and yellow blossoms and looks like a pineapple. It grows in Arizona and New Mexico.

The sunset pincushion, which also grows in Arizona and New Mexico, is a little smaller, with pink or rose blossoms.

The foxtail pincushion, which is found in Arizona, California, and Nevada, is a small, roundish, or cylinder-shaped plant. It has white spines. Each spine has a red or brown tip, which makes the whole plant, from a distance, look like a fox's tail. The flowers are straw colored.

The fish-hook pincushion may be a foot in height. This round cactus has tubercles and white thorns, and one or more hooked spines. The flowers are purple. It is common in the Southwest.

The smallest of all the pincushions is the Arizona pincushion, which is no more than an inch high and an inch wide. It grows in the Grand Canyon.

The Mexican pincushion, often seen in cactus gardens, is found in our Southwest. It is a low plant with gray-white spines.

Some other pincushions, with greenish-yellow flowers, grow in the plains north from Texas to Missouri, Kansas, and Montana. The snowball pincushion, which is covered with white spines, is a prairie cactus found in Texas and north into Kansas and Colorado, and into Canada. Its flowers are pink or purple.

Two kinds of pincushion cacti are on the Smithsonian list of commercially exploited plants: *Mammillaria orestera*, from

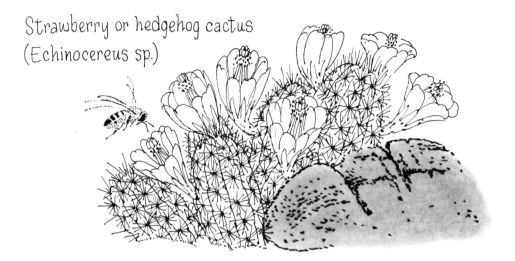

Strawberry or hedgehog cactus
(Echinocereus sp.)

Arizona and New Mexico, and *Mammillaria thornberi* from Arizona. They are being dug up too often by people who sell cactus plants.

And as we have said, no rare cactus plants should be removed from the habitat where they grow naturally. They should be left to grow where they do best, in the wild.

HEDGEHOG CACTUS, STRAWBERRY CACTUS

Another plant often seen in cactus gardens is the hedgehog cactus (genus *Echinocereus*). It is also called the strawberry cactus because the masses of fruit are red in color and look like strawberries.

There are sixty species of hedgehog cactus growing wild from Kansas, Oklahoma, and Texas west into California.

Some hedgehog cacti are up to twelve inches high. They have

fluted stems, covered with spines. The fruits, which are good to eat, are also covered with spines, but the spines are easily rubbed off. The flowers are red, purple, or yellow. The hedgehog cacti often grow in large clumps, with over a hundred plants in one clump.

Four kinds of hedgehog cactus are on the Smithsonian endangered list in Texas, and one each in Arizona, California, New

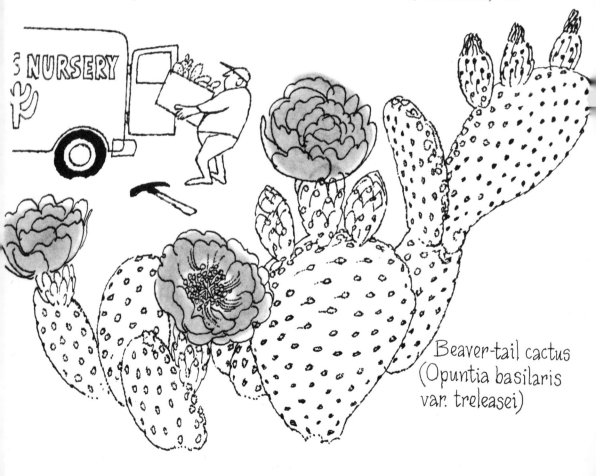

Beaver-tail cactus
(Opuntia basilaris
var. treleasei)

Mexico, and Utah. Three varieties from Texas are threatened; also one in Arizona and one in California.

Three species of hedgehog catcus are being overcollected from the wild by plant dealers and have been placed on the Smithsonian list of commercially exploited species.

PRICKLY PEAR AND CANE (CHOLLA) CACTUS

There are about 130 species of these cacti (genus *Opuntia*). The spines are painful to touch.

The stems and the flat pads of the prickly pear are prickly indeed. Prickly pears often grow in low mats on the ground. The flowers are yellow, red, or purple and measure two or three inches across. The fruit, from one to three inches long, is barrel shaped and red or sometimes yellow in color. Also called Indian fig, the fruit may be eaten raw or stewed, and is sometimes made into preserves and cactus candy.

The eastern prickly pear (*Opuntia humifusa*) is the only cactus found wild in New York state. It also grows in Massachusetts and north into Ontario, Canada, south into Alabama and Florida, and west into Missouri. It can also be found in the Southwest. It grows on rocks and sand dunes, and on beaches and sandy prairies.

Cholla is the Spanish word for cane cactus. The stems of cane cacti are spiny canes. Cane cacti may be up to fifteen to twenty feet high. They often grow in hedges in the Southwest, where they are common.

One endangered prickly pear (*Opuntia basilaris* var. *treleasei*), also called beaver-tail cactus, grows in California and Arizona. It is a low, spreading plant, rarely a foot high, and has purple or sometimes white flowers that are three inches in diameter.

Four other species of *Opuntia* are threatened in California, four in Arizona, two kinds in Texas and two kinds in Florida, and one each in Nevada and Utah.

Another *Opuntia* (*Opuntia strigil* var. *flexospina*) was last collected in Texas in 1911, and is believed to be gone forever. It is extinct.

Protected Giant Saguaro

The saguaro (also spelled *sahuaro*) *Carnegiea gigantea* is our biggest cactus. It may grow up to sixty feet high. Hawks build nests in the forks of this tree cactus. Owls and woodpeckers nest in holes in the stems.

The saguaro is not endangered, because it is protected by state and federal governments. It is included here as an example of a protected plant.

The giant saguaro is one of the oldest living plants. A plant alive today may be two hundred years old. This means that it

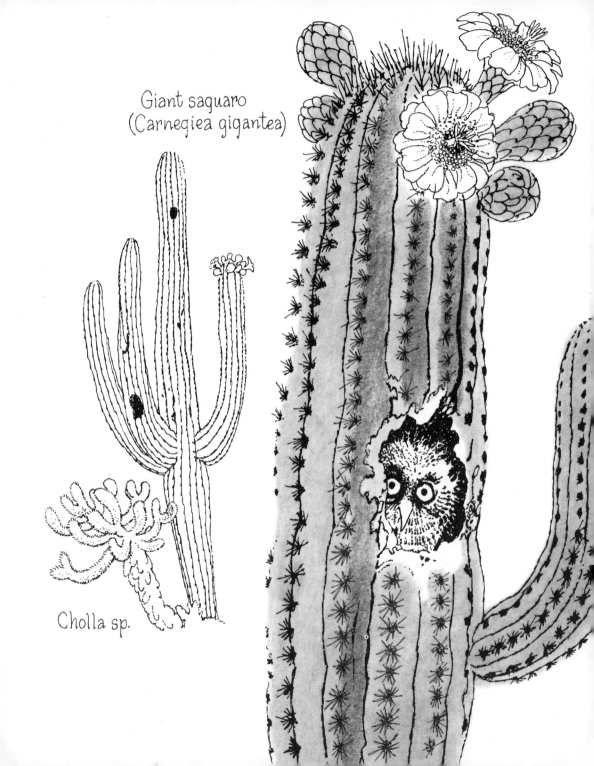

Giant saguaro
(Carnegiea gigantea)

Cholla sp.

was a seedling when the American Revolutionary War started in 1776.

It is the state flower of Arizona, where most saguaros grow. A few grow wild in California. This cactus is particularly well protected in the Saguaro National Forest, Tucson, Arizona, on 2,000 acres of desert land.

When rain comes to the desert, the huge, fluted stems of the saguaro fill up and swell. When there is no rain, the stems shrink and wrinkle. A saguaro can survive three years without rain.

The white flower is about four inches long. The red or purple fruit is edible, and may be eaten raw. It is also made into cactus candy and preserves.

Now, what can you do to help save the cactus plants?

We repeat, do not remove any cactus plants growing in the wild.

Suppose that you want to buy a potted cactus plant. Should you? Yes, if you go to a dealer who does not take his plants from the wild. Ask your dealer if his plants are raised from seeds. Some cactus dealers raise plants from seeds that they collect from their own plants. These dealers are trying to save the plants that are growing in the wild. (See Appendix 2 for a list of some of the cactus dealers who raise their plants from seeds.)

And seed-grown plants do better indoors than plants brought in from the wild.

American ginseng
(Panax quinquefolius)

American Ginseng

American ginseng (*Panax quinquefolius*) is a wild plant growing in hardwood forests from Canada south to northern Florida and Alabama and west to Louisiana and Arkansas. It is small, up to about fifteen inches high. Each stem is topped by a whorl of leaves. The short flower stalk rises a little above the leaves with a cluster of small, yellowish-green flowers. It blooms in mid-summer. The berries are red and appear in the late summer and fall.

In five-year-old plants, the roots are from two to four inches long, and up to an inch thick. And at five years and older, the roots are usually forked, and look like a man's body and legs.

The true ginseng (*Panax schinseng*) grows in southeast Asia, China, Korea, and the Soviet Far East. There the root is used as a medicine. So much of this ginseng root is used in the Orient that there is not enough for the market.

Also, American ginseng is now planted and grown in gardens, orchards, and woods in the United States for shipment to China. And great numbers of American ginseng plants are removed from the wild and shipped to China.

23

Do not dig up any ginseng plants. The wild American ginseng is becoming rare.

Among other plants that are overdug by plant dealers and private collectors, and are threatened or endangered, are the interesting and strange Venus fly trap and pitcher plants. These plants use insects for food.

Venus's Flytrap

The Venus's flytrap (*Dionaea muscipula*) is a small plant that grows in sandy bogs in North and South Carolina. Each plant has four to eight basal leaves, which form a rosette on the soil.

Each leaf is from one to five inches long. The tip end of the leaf is divided into two halves. This is the flytrap. There are bristles on the edge of each leaf half. On the inner surface are three short, stiff hairs. When an insect lands on these hairs, the leaf snaps shut. The bristles lock. The insect is trapped and "eaten." Juices in this part of the leaf digest the insect.

In the month of May the flower stalk of the Venus's flytrap grows up to ten inches high. In June from four to ten white flowers bloom.

Parrot pitcher plant
(Sarracenia psittacina)

Venus's flytrap
(Dionaea muscipula)

This member of the family Droseraceae is threatened in both North and South Carolina. It is now protected by state law in North Carolina.

Pitcher Plant

Pitcher plants are bog plants (family Sarraceniaceae).

The flower of the common pitcher plant (*Sarracenia purpurea*) is usually purple. When growing in a sunny place, it is some-

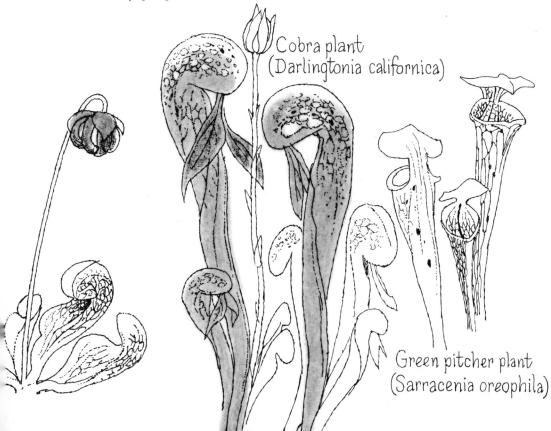

Cobra plant
(*Darlingtonia californica*)

Green pitcher plant
(*Sarracenia oreophila*)

times green or red. The leaves, which come from the base of the plant, are up to eight inches long and shaped like a pitcher. This gives the plant its name.

Inside the pitchers are nectar glands that attract insects. The pitchers are usually partly filled with rain water. Stiff hairs line the inside of the pitcher and point downward. Insects are attracted to the nectar. It is easy for an insect to crawl over the downturned hairs, into the pitcher. But once in, it is difficult for the wet insect to crawl out over the hairs. The pitcher plant uses the drowned insects as food.

The common pitcher plant is found from Labrador west to the Rocky Mountains and south to Florida. It is not yet endangered or threatened.

The green pitcher plant (*Sarracenia oreophila*) is endangered. It grows in Tennessee, Alabama, and Georgia.

Several other pitcher plants are threatened and all are commercially exploited. One, called the cobra plant (*Darlingtonia californica*), grows in California and Oregon. Another, the parrot pitcher plant (*Sarracenia psittacina*), comes from Alabama, Florida, Georgia, Mississippi, and Louisana. And a third threatened species, the sweet pitcher plant (*Sarracenia rubra*), also grows in the Deep South.

Tiburon Mariposa lily
(Calochortus tiburonensis)

Mariposa Lily

These beautiful members of the lily family (Liliaceae) grow from bulbs on dry mountain slopes in western America. There are forty to fifty species. They have slender stems and usually only one flower to a plant with white, yellow, rose, or lilac petals. Mariposa is the Spanish word meaning butterfly.

Since Mariposa lilies grow well in gardens and in flower pots, they are in danger of being dug up to the point of extinction in the wild.

Three kinds of Mariposa lilies (genus *Calochortus*) are endangered in California. Seven other species of *Calochortus* are on the Smithsonian threatened list in five states in the Far West.

And one is believed to be extinct in California.

Very Rare Panamint Daisy

The threatened panamint daisy (*Enceliopsis covillei*) belongs to the sunflower family (Asteraceae). It has beautiful golden-yellow flowers.

27

Panamint daisy
(Enceliopsis covillei)

Stonecrop
(Sedum nevii)

This handsome plant grows in a difficult climate. It is found on the western slopes of the Panamint Mountains in southeastern California, west of Death Valley, at an altitude of from 1,200 to 4,000 feet.

Wild burros that are descended from the burros let loose by gold prospectors years ago feed on this rare daisy.

The panamint daisy has been chosen as the symbol of the California Native Plant Society.

Close relatives of the panamint daisy in California and Nevada are threatened also.

Sedum

Sedums (family Crassulaceae), also called stonecrop, are little perennial evergreen plants with small, fleshy leaves. They are found in sandy, rocky places and are most common in the cooler regions though some are found in the South. Most kinds like the sun, a few grow in shade.

Sedum comes from the Latin word meaning "to sit," which

sedums do. It is a good name for these plants. So, too, is the name *stonecrop*, for these little plants attach themselves to the rocky ledges where they grow.

The clusters of flowers of most sedums are white. Some are yellow or purple.

People like to grow sedums in rock gardens, and some are in danger of being overcollected by commercial and private pickers.

Three sedums are on the Smithsonian endangered list: *Sedum texanum* in Texas, *Sedum nevii* in Alabama and Tennessee, and *Sedum rosea* var. *roanensis* in North Carolina and Tennessee. Four are on the threatened list: *Sedum laxum* ssp. *heckneri* in Oregon and California; *Sedum niveum* in California; *Sedum pusillum* in Arkansas, Georgia, North Carolina, and South Carolina; and *Sedum robertsianum*, in Texas.

Starry Grasswort

Starry grasswort (*Cerastium arvense* var. *villosissimum*) is a form of chickweed (family Caryophyllaceae). It is a perennial with low, matted branches. The eight- to twelve-inch stems have pale green leaves. The numerous white flowers blossom in April and May.

Variety *villosissimum* grows in Pennsylvania, and is endangered.

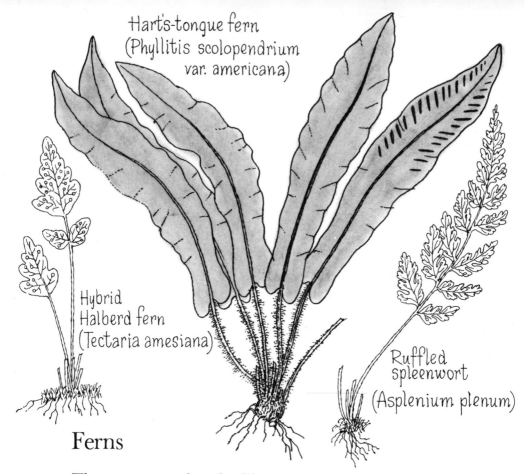

Hart's-tongue fern
(Phyllitis scolopendrium
var. americana)

Hybrid
Halberd fern
(Tectaria amesiana)

Ruffled
spleenwort
(Asplenium plenum)

Ferns

There are many fern families. Ferns have beautiful leaves but they have no flowers or seeds. They reproduce by spores.

A fern spore is a special cell. Spores develop in structures that are tightly clustered together on the underside of the fern leaf or frond. These clusters, known as sori, are sometimes called fruit dots. Eventually the spores drop to the ground. When the temperature is right, and rain comes, the spores develop into little new ferns.

30

Curly grass fern
(Schizaea germanii)

Ferns vary in size from tiny, creeping plants to tropical tree ferns that are up to eighty feet in height with stems almost a foot in diameter.

POLYPODY FERN

The polypody ferns belong to the largest of the true fern families (family Polypodiaceae). Those in the genus *Polypodium* are rugged and coarse, and are mostly evergreen. They grow in clusters from short, scaly underground stems called rhizomes. The narrow leaves are widest at the middle. They are sometimes picked for greenery at Christmas time, which has given them the name of Christmas ferns. These ferns live and stay green all year round on snow-covered ground on rocky hillsides.

One of the polypody family (*Polystichum kruckebergii*) is on the Smithsonian list of threatened ferns being gathered too much by plant dealers and by private collectors in the state of Washington.

Another polypody fern (*Grammitis nimbata*) is on the endangered list in the state of North Carolina. Hart's-tongue fern (*Phyllitis scolopendrium* var. *americana*) is endangered in Michigan, New York, and Tennessee. And a fourth, *Woodsia abbeae*, appears on the endangered list in Minnesota, Wisconsin, and Michigan.

31

Eleven more species of the polypody family are on the threatened list in the continental United States, according to the Smithsonian report:

Asplenium ebenoides   Alabama, New Jersey, Ohio, Pennsylvania, Virginia, West Virginia

Asplenium heteroresiliens   Georgia, North Carolina, South Carolina

Asplenium kentuckiense   Arkansas, Illinois, Kentucky, Ohio, Virginia

Asplenium plenum   Florida

Cheilanthes fibrillosa   California

Cheilanthes pringlei   Arizona

Cheilanthes pyramidalis var. *arizonica*   Arizona

Gymnocarpium heterosporum   Alaska, Michigan, Minnesota, Wisconsin

Notholaena lemmoni   Arizona, New Mexico

Notholaena schaffneri var. *nealleyi*   Texas

Tectaria amesiana   Florida

CURLY GRASS FERN

This family of ferns (Schizaeaceae) looks very un-fernlike. Small and only a few inches tall, the curly grass ferns seem more like grasses than ferns. There are about twenty-nine species. They grow in wet soil and bogs and swamps.

One threatened curly grass fern (*Schizaea pusilla*) may be found in New Jersey and New York. And an endangered species (*Schizaea germanii*) is native to Florida.

Roadsides

A great deal of land is used for building roads. There are many miles of roads in and around every little town in America. Thousands upon thousands more run between towns and cities. Of course city areas are so paved that few areas can be planted.

Country roadsides are a fine place for wild flowers and shrubs to live if they are allowed to grow undisturbed. To keep roadsides open, however, some towns spray with herbicides which kill all of the beautiful wild flowers and woody plants. When roadsides are mowed to keep them open, wild flowers may continue to grow there but they cannot go to seed.

Among the common flowers growing along country roadsides are goldenrods, thistles, and milkweeds.

GOLDENROD

Goldenrod is a beautiful wild flower of the family Compositae, called family Asteraceae in recent books. There are some eighty-five species found in the northern United States and in parts of

33

the South. This perennial has slender stems up to eight feet high and small clusters of lovely, golden-yellow flowers. There is one white-flowered species, called silver-rod.

Goldenrods grow along roadsides, in swamps, and in moist woods and thickets. They bloom from late summer into October.

Though often called a weed, goldenrod is very popular. It is the official flower of two states, Kentucky and Nebraska.

Some of the goldenrods are common but others are rare.

Three species of goldenrod are on the Smithsonian endangered list: *Solidago albopilosa* in Kentucky; *Solidago lindheimeriana* in Texas; and *Solidago shortii* in Kentucky and Ohio. Two are on the threatened list: *Solidago mollis* var. *angustata* in Texas; *Solidago spithamaea* in Alabama, North Carolina, and Tennessee.

Milkweed
(Asclepias
meadii)

Goldenrod
(Solidago shortii)

Thistles also belong to the family Compositae (Asteraceae).

The common Canada thistle is a well-known weed from coast to coast in the United States. It has spiny leaves and lilac, magenta, or, rarely, white flowers and grows from one to three feet high. Its silky-haired seeds are blown about by wind into gardens, lawns, and fields, and along roadsides. Like many other thistles growing in America, the Canada thistle came here from Europe.

A few thistles are native to the midwestern and western states. Three of them, *Cirsium fontinale* var. *fontinale, Cirsium loncholepis,* and *Cirsium rohthophilum,* are endangered in California, and one, *Cirsium clokeyi,* is endangered in Nevada.

MILKWEED, SILKWEED

There are about eighty species of milkweed, most of them in North America. They belong to the family Asclepiadaceae.

The plants have a milky juice and pretty flower clusters, and hairy leaves and stems. Stout pods, about four inches long, contain the seeds. Each seed has a tuft of silky hairs at one end. This is why the plants are often called silkweeds.

The common milkweed (*Asclepias syriaca*) grows to a height of five feet. It lives along roadsides and in fields in Canada from

35

New Brunswick west to Saskatchewan, and in the United States as far south as North Carolina, and west to Kansas.

There is one species of milkweed (*Asclepias eastwoodiana*) endangered in Nevada.

Four are on the threatened list: *Asclepias cutleri* in Arizona and Utah; *Asclepias meadii* in Illinois, Indiana, Iowa, Kansas, and Missouri; *Asclepias ruthiae* in Utah; and *Asclepias viridula* in Florida.

Out on the Prairie

The grassy prairie is the home of many lovely wild flowers. But thousands of acres of prairie land have been plowed up to plant wheat and corn and other crops. The wild plants growing there are disappearing.

Great herds of sheep and cattle are grazed on the prairie and plains. The sheep and cattle eat the endangered as well as the common wild flowers.

Among the endangered flowers on the prairie is the pretty shooting star.

French's shooting star
(Dodecatheon frenchii)

SHOOTING STAR

This plant of the primrose family (Primulaceae) is called the shooting star because of the shape of its flower. The stamens, where pollen is made, form a point in front of the petals which thus seem to follow behind it, giving the effect of a shooting star.

The common shooting star is up to two feet high. The flowers are purple-pink or yellow-white in color. It grows on prairies, and also on hillsides, cliffs, and in the woods. It is found from Pennsylvania south to Georgia and west to South Dakota and Texas.

Other shooting stars are found over most of the United States. The threatened French's shooting star (*Dodecatheon frenchii*) grows in Arkansas, Kentucky, and Illinois. Another, *Dodecatheon poeticum,* is threatened in Washington and Oregon.

37

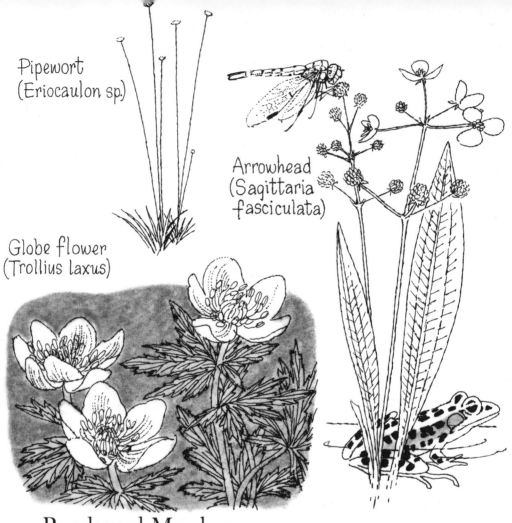

Pipewort
(Eriocaulon sp.)

Arrowhead
(Saqittaria
fasciculata)

Globe flower
(Trollius laxus)

Ponds and Marshes

In other areas in the country, people are building dams and
flooding thousands of acres of land. All of the wild plants die.
They are drowned.

Of course many kinds of plants, such as pond lilies, live in water. Many other plants grow in marshy places. Some of these are endangered.

ARROWHEAD

The pretty arrowhead plants belong to the water plantain family (Alismataceae). They have white flowers, and grow up to four feet tall. Named for their arrow-shaped leaves, they are found in bogs and shallow ponds in North America.

One species, *Sagittaria fasciculata,* is endangered in North Carolina.

GLOBE FLOWER

Beautiful globe-shaped flowers of the family Ranunculaceae are found in marshy places in the United States. There are a dozen or more species. The slender stems are up to two feet long, and sometimes turn upward. The large white, yellow, or purple flowers are one to two inches across. They bloom in the spring or early summer.

One species, *Trollius laxus,* is endangered in the states of Connecticut, Delaware, Maine, Michigan, New Hampshire, New Jersey, Ohio, and Pennsylvania.

PIPEWORT

Pipeworts (family Eriocaulaceae) are water plants with grasslike leaves and long, stiff flower stalks. The small white flowers blossom above the water level.

One of the species, *Eriocaulon kornickianum,* is on the endangered list in Texas, Arkansas, and Oklahoma.

MONKEY FLOWER

Monkey flowers belong to the snapdragon family (Scrophulariaceae). They can be found in swamps and wet meadows and beside rivers and ponds. They have square, upright stems that grow from one to three feet high. The flowers, which are purple, are shaped so that they look like monkeys grinning. In fact the Latin name for the genus, *mimulus,* means "little buffoon." Monkey flowers blossom from June to September.

The common monkey flower (*Mimulus ringens*) is found in northeastern and north-central North America.

Mimulus ringens var. *colpophilus* is an endangered monkey flower that grows only in the state of Maine. *Mimulus glabratus* var. *michiganensis* is on the endangered list in the state of Michigan. *Mimulus guttatus* ssp. *arenicola* is found in California, where it is endangered.

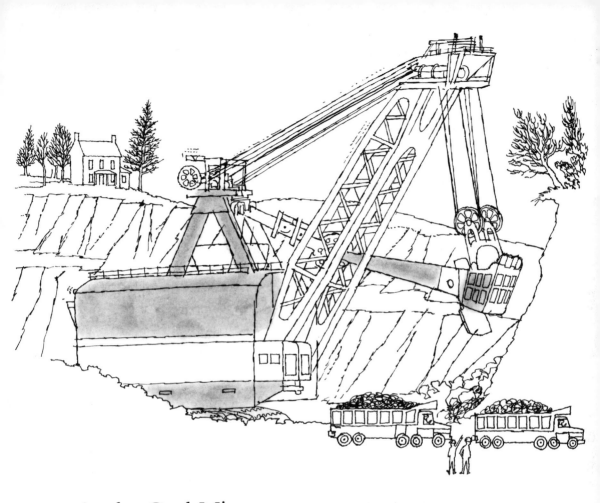

At the Coal Mines

Mining is an activity which can threaten the lives of flowers, shrubs, and trees.

Coal is mined not only from deep pits but also from the surface of the ground. This is called strip mining. Half of the coal used in America comes from these surface mines.

This means that earth and rocks are removed to uncover the coal, which lies near the surface.

In flat areas, the miners use giant earth-moving machines to plow away soil. These giant machines can move several thousand cubic yards of earth in an hour. Where they have worked, no living plants are left, and no soil in which seeds may grow.

In the mountains often a whole mountain top, including the plants growing there, is removed.

In some states there is now a law that plowed soil at surface mines must be kept in pits and returned to the mined area after the mining is finished. First the subsoil (poor soil, often mixed with rocks) is returned. Then the good soil is spread, on top. And the area is replanted.

This is a big step in helping both endangered and common wild flowers, shrubs, and trees to continue to grow, as they did before people began digging up the earth to get coal.

A Copper Mine in the Desert

There is an open-pit copper mine in the desert in Arizona where native shrubs and trees are being replanted. This is a good example of what should be done at all mines. Material taken from the mine is kept and returned to the land. Good topsoil is spread over that.

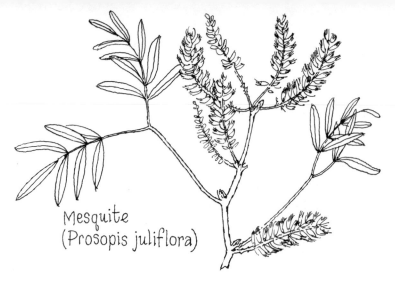

Mesquite
(Prosopis juliflora)

Native plants are set out and watered until they take hold. Among the common native plants there is mesquite (*Prosopis juliflora*). Mesquite is a shrub or tree growing usually twenty feet high, sometimes up to fifty feet. It has a pair of sharp spines where the leaves join the stem. The flowers are greenish-white. The pods are used for baking a sweet cake. Since the roots of this desert tree go down fifty feet to find water, mesquite will survive when established without further care.

Fire in a Forest

At another location, this time in a forest, a careless camper drops a lighted match. Fire roars through the forest, killing many living plants. A forest fire burns whole trees, trunks, branches, twigs, leaves or needles, and also the underbrush, and any wild plants growing under the trees. Many tree seeds, however, live and are able to send up seedlings after the fire; and sprouts also come from the tree roots.

But the land, burned bare, washes badly, that is, erodes, and the plant foods found in the soil are carried away.

Many fires are started by lightning but more are started by people. In 1973 in the National Forests alone 6,048 fires were caused by people.

Smokey the Bear, the character who appears on posters in outdoor areas, is a well-known symbol of those who are working to prevent forest fires, set by people.

Clear Cutting

In another spot, also in a forest, along come men with power saws. They cut and cut. They harvest the trees for use as lumber and firewood. They cut down all of the trees, every single one.

Clear cutting causes bad erosion of the soil on steep land that has little ground cover (plants growing under the trees). In less steep country, the branches left behind prevent bad erosion. Some trees come again from the tree roots and seeds. But clear cutting removes the shade needed by some plants and exposes them to the sun. And sun-loving weeds invade the cleared area and choke out the native plants.

The worst damage in forests is caused by roads built by

loggers for traveling and for hauling away logs. These roads, particularly the roads along which logs are dragged, cause bad erosion. Rains come and the roads wash, taking away soil and tree food (nutrients in the soil) and tree seeds.

Wilderness and Primitive Areas

The best method of protecting and saving wild plants—trees as well as wild flowers—is to let them grow in their own natural home. This is a better and surer way than growing seedlings in a garden and then replanting them in the wild. Many wild plants do not transplant well.

A good example of how the United States government is saving trees and other plants in the wild may be seen in the Wilderness and Primitive Areas of the National Forests.

Would you like to hike, or paddle your canoe, or ride your horse or burro, and camp in the real wilderness? We mean the wilderness the way it was long ago when the first settlers came from Europe to America. We mean the deep forest where trees and flowering plants grow as they did when America was discovered, where there are no towns, only wild country inhabited by rabbits and hares, bighorn mountain sheep, mountain goats, bears, mountain lions, great eagles and condors, and other kinds of beasts and birds.

45

When the Pilgrims came to America, trees covered one half of the American continent. Today, forest covers one third of the country. And you can still see the real wilderness in some of our National Forests, where many acres have been set aside as Wilderness and Primitive Areas. Members of the Forest Service manage the areas.

No automobiles are allowed, except now and again for use by foresters in emergencies.

There are no roads except where necessary in some places where there are mines, or where there is land owned by individuals.

No cutting of trees for lumber is allowed.

The only buildings are fire lookout towers, a few cabins where people own land, and a few work rooms for foresters who manage the forests. The foresters usually camp out, and ride a horse or walk, as you and I must if we visit. In general you may camp where you wish. But check with the local forest ranger on the area where you expect to go, to make sure there are no restrictions. In a few places it is dangerous to start camp fires.

You may pick wild fruit and nuts to eat. But you cannot pick or dig up any plants to take away with you.

There are eighty-eight Wilderness and Primitive Areas in fourteen western states, including the first area that was established in the Gila National Forest in New Mexico. In these Wilderness and Primitive Areas are 14.3 million acres of forest land where you can go backpacking, or riding, or paddling your canoe. And you will find good fishing and hunting, which are allowed in these areas subject to local state game laws.

These areas offer a wonderful opportunity to study and photograph both the endangered and common varieties of big trees and shrubs and flowers in our western woods.

Our National Forests

The Forest Service manages 155 National Forests and 19 National Grasslands in 44 states, Puerto Rico, and the Virgin Islands. There are 187 million acres of land in the National Forests.

Within the National Forests, timber is sold by the government and harvested by private lumber companies. After the trees are cut, they are replaced with seedlings that are properly planted. In 1973, 639 million trees were raised and planted by foresters of the Forest Service and of the states where the forests are located.

Anyone who wishes to take plants from these well-managed National Forests must have a special written permit. Many endangered and threatened plants survive in National Forests, and also in National Parks.

The Forest Service also oversees 3.8 million acres of National Grasslands. It sells to ranchers the right to graze their sheep and cattle in the Grasslands.

All this, plus the fun of hiking, backpacking, riding, and camping are yours to enjoy in the National Forests.

Some of the wild flowers that you will find growing in the National Forests, and in woods in other parts of the country, are trilliums, columbine, and gentians. Each of these lovely groups includes some endangered and threatened species.

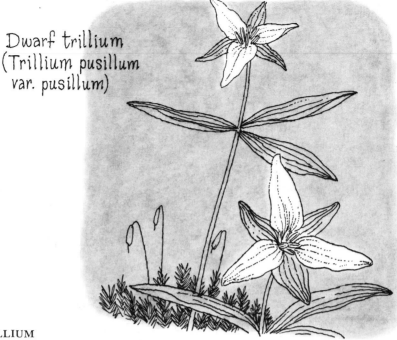

Dwarf trillium
(Trillium pusillum
var. pusillum)

TRILLIUM

Trilliums are showy wild flowers that belong to the family
Liliaceae. About thirty species grow in the North American
woods. Each plant has three leaves and a single flower. Each
flower has three petals. The name trillium is from the Latin
triplum which means triple, or in threes. Certain trilliums are
also called wake robins.

In some kinds, the stout flower stalk is only six inches high;
in others it is up to eighteen inches. The berries are red.

Trillium undulatum can be found in the woods of the North.
Trillium grandiflorum grows in woods from Canada to the
mountains of North Carolina and Florida and west to beyond

49

the Great Lakes. Another species, *Trillium rivale,* is found in woods of the mountains of California and Oregon.

One trillium (*Trillium pusillum* var. *virginianum*) is on the endangered list in Virginia and Maryland. Another (*Trillium pusillum* var. *pusillum*) is on the threatened list in North and South Carolina. A third (*Trillium pusillum* var. *ozarkanum*) is on the threatened list in Arkansas and Missouri. A fourth (*Trillium texanum*) is on the threatened list in Texas.

COLUMBINE

Columbine is a beautiful perennial flower of the buttercup family (Ranunculaceae). The common kind (*Aquilegia canadensis*) is about one to two feet high and has red and yellow flowers with long nectar spurs. It grows in rocky places and rich woods in the eastern states and in the Rocky Mountains.

One variety (*Aquilegia canadensis* var. *australis*) is on the Smithsonian endangered list in Florida. Another kind (*Aquilegia jonesii*) with blue flowers, is found only in Wyoming and Montana, where it is on the threatened list. It is also on the list of commercially exploited plants dug up and carried away by plant sellers.

Aquilegia chaplinei is on the endangered list in Texas and New Mexico. *Aquilegia hinckleyana* is endangered in Texas. *Aquilegia micrantha* var. *mancosana* is endangered in Colorado.

50

GENTIAN

There are about three dozen species of the gentian family (Gentianaceae) in the eastern, southern, and central states, and some on the Pacific Coast. They are mostly blue-flowered alpine plants, living at high altitudes.

The most famous is the fringed gentian (*Gentiana crinita*). It grows from one to two feet high, and has beautiful vase-shaped, fringed blue flowers. It is found in moist woods and meadows from Maine to the Dakotas, south to Iowa and, in the mountains, to Georgia. The fringed gentian is not now endangered but do not pick it or dig it up.

There are seven endangered members of the gentian family: *Bartonia texana* in Texas; *Centaurium namophilum* in California and Nevada; *Frasera gypsicola* in Nevada and Utah; *Frasera pahutensis* in Nevada; *Gentiana bisetaea* in Oregon; *Gentiana deloachii* in Georgia; and *Gentiana pennelliana* in Florida.

Six more of the gentians are on the threatened list.

Gentiana bisetaea

American chestnut
(Castanea dentata)

Shrubs and Trees

Let us turn now for a look at the big plants growing in the wild, the shrubs and trees. There follows a description of some of those that are endangered or threatened, and a few that are very rare but so well protected that they are surviving.

AMERICAN CHESTNUT

The American chestnut (*Castanea dentata*) is a tree found from Maine, New Hampshire, and Vermont west to Michigan and Indiana, south to Delaware and along the Allegheny Mountains to Kentucky, Tennessee, Alabama, and Mississippi. It is famous for its good-tasting nuts. The nuts, enclosed in a spiny burr that is two or three inches in diameter, are usually three in number.

The American chestnuts are or rather *were*, big trees, from sixty to ninety feet high, with a trunk diameter of three to five feet. Sometimes a tree would reach a height of 120 feet, and a diameter of seven feet.

Chestnuts were valuable lumber trees. In 1909, 663 million board feet of lumber were taken from these trees. The lumber was used for house construction but more often for making furniture and boxes, telephone poles, crossties for railroads, fence posts, and shingles, and for fuel and pulpwood (for making paper). The wood was also a source of tannin, for tanning leather. In the year 1923, 55,301 tons of tannin were produced from American chestnut wood.

By 1940 nearly all American chestnut trees had been killed by a fungus (*Endothia parasitica*), which first came to America about 1900.

Actually the American chestnut trees are not all dead. Some of them continue to sprout from stumps and roots and bear flowers but eventually they die from the fungus. So the American chestnut is no longer an important forest tree.

Foresters are now trying to breed American chestnut trees that are immune to the chestnut blight and thus bring back this great tree.

FLORIDA YEW

The yews (family Taxaceae) are evergreen trees but do not bear cones as most evergreens do. Instead the seeds are in the fleshy, red, berrylike fruit. The seeds, wood, bark, and leaves are poisonous if eaten.

The very rare Florida yew (*Taxus floridana*) grows mostly along the east bank of the Apalachicola River in northwestern Florida. Some small plants have been set out in the National Arboretum in Washington, D.C.

The Florida yew is from ten to eighteen feet high. It is found only in Florida and is on the endangered list there.

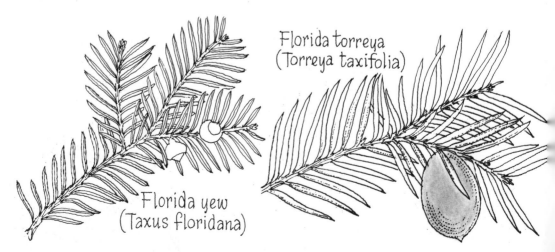

Florida torreya
(Torreya taxifolia)

Florida yew
(Taxus floridana)

FLORIDA TORREYA

Another rare tree is the Florida torreya (*Torreya taxifolia*), an ornamental evergreen of the yew family. Reaching up to forty feet high, with spreading branches, it has purple fruit that is one to one and a half inches long.

It is protected in the Torreya State Park in Florida, and a few seedlings are growing in the National Arboretum. It is endangered in Florida and Georgia, where it is highly subject to fungus disease.

GEORGIA PLUME

The Georgia plume (*Elliottia racemosa*) is a rare endangered shrub of the heath family (Ericaceae). This shrub grows from four to ten, sometimes up to twenty, feet high, and has beautiful white flowers. It is found in wet, sandy woods in Georgia. It is deciduous, that is, it sheds its leaves in the fall of the year.

Georgia plume
(Elliottia racemosa)

AMERICAN ELM

Of the different kinds of elm trees found in North America, the most important is the American elm (*Ulmus americana*), which grows from Newfoundland west through Canada to the Rocky Mountains and south to Texas and Florida. It is a handsome tree, from eighty to over one hundred feet high. The crown spreads in the shape of a vase. It is valued as a shade and ornamental tree, and is often planted along the streets of towns and cities because of its beauty.

The elm is also a famous historic tree.

THE LIBERTY TREE

In 1646, the citizens of Boston planted elms along the Boston Common. Over a hundred years later, the descendants of the elm tree planters were angry about the Stamp Act, which the British Parliament passed in 1765 to tax Americans in the colonies. Patriots calling themselves Free Men and the Sons of Liberty gathered under one of these trees and hanged an effigy of Lord John Stuart Bute, who originated the Stamp Act. They also hanged an effigy of the local stamp distributor, Andrew Oliver. This tree was called the Liberty Tree and was a gathering place for patriots until the British soldiers burned it down in 1775..

The American Elm Institute of New Hampshire has urged

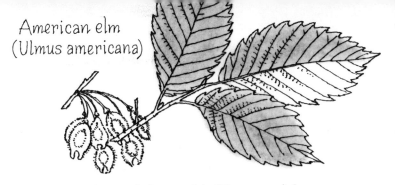

American elm
(Ulmus americana)

people to plant "Liberty Trees" to celebrate the Bicentennial, 330 years after the planting of the first elm trees in Boston. The Elm Institute asks people to gather seeds from their elms, dry them, and send them to the Institute where they are planted and raised. The young seedlings are then sold at a very low price to schools and to people who would like to grow these beautiful and historic trees.

Not so important as a forest tree, elm wood is used for making plywood, furniture, boxes, and pulp for paper.

Unfortunately the American elm is attacked by several insects and diseases. The worst disease is the Dutch elm disease, a fungus (*Ceratocystis ulmi*) which was brought into the United States about 1930. The fungus is carried from tree to tree by elm bark beetles. Although great numbers of elms have died in the East and Middle West, the trees are still here. Foresters are getting rid of the bark beetles by luring them into traps baited with odors the beetles like, the smell of elm wood and the odor of a female bark beetle to attract the male beetles. In the Detroit area, 1,100 traps caught 3 million beetles.

Now a company is making a fungicide for control of the Dutch elm disease in the United States.

The best known of the handsome maple trees, and not in danger, is the sugar maple (*Acer saccharum*). A big tree, it grows from seventy to one hundred feet tall. The sap is used for making maple sugar.

The smaller, and very rare, Uvalde bigtooth maple (*Acergrandidentatum* var. *sinuosum*) is threatened. It grows to about forty feet high and is found only on the Edwards Plateau in central Texas.

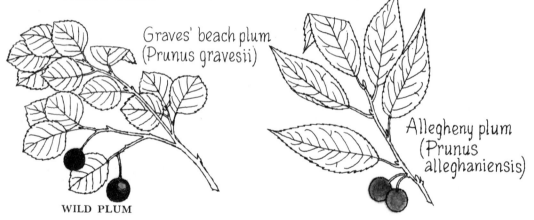

Graves' beach plum
(Prunus gravesii)

Allegheny plum
(Prunus
alleghaniensis)

WILD PLUM

The beach or shore plums (family Rosaceae) grow on the eastern seashore and some miles inland. The straggling bushes, some of which are thorny, have small white flowers and purple fruit, about a half inch in diameter. The plums make good jelly and preserves.

One endangered species (*Prunus gravesii*) is a small bushy beach plum about three feet high which grows only around Groton, Connecticut, near Long Island Sound. It has dark, rough bark. Another species (*Prunus geniculata*), found in Florida, is also endangered.

The Allegheny plum (*Prunus alleghaniensis*) is a small bush or tree from twelve to fifteen feet high with few, if any, thorns. The plums are used for making preserves and pie. It grows in Connecticut, Pennsylvania, and West Virginia, and is threatened in all these states.

The creek plum (*Prunus texana*), of the prairies of Texas, is a shrub up to eight feet high. Growing densely, it forms thickets. The small red fruit ripens in June. It, too, is threatened.

Other species threatened in Texas are the Havard plum (*Prunus havardii*) and *Prunus minutiflora* and *Prunus murrayana*.

LAUREL

Native laurels are handsome shrubs. Found in rocky woods and hilly or mountainous country, they grow from Canada south to the Gulf of Mexico. The mountain laurel (*Kalmia latifolia*) has beautiful evergreen leaves and white, pink-tinged, sometimes deep pink, flowers. It grows from four up to occasionally thirty-eight feet high.

White wicky
(Kalmia cuneata)

One endangered species of laurel, the white wicky (*Kalmia cuneata*), a small shrub up to four feet high, has white flowers with a red band within. It blossoms in June and is not an evergreen. It is one of the rarest shrubs in the United States, and is found only in North and South Carolina.

A word of warning. Common names of plants can be confusing and sometimes dangerous. The leaves, twigs, and flowers of species of the wild laurel (genus *Kalmia,* family Ericaceae) are very poisonous to eat.

On the other hand, another plant or rather tree, the bay laurel, also called the sweet bay tree, from which we get our edible bay leaves for cooking, belongs to an entirely different family.

The bay laurel (*Laurus nobilis*) is a member of the true laurel family (Lauraceae), and is native to the Mediterranean region. It is now often grown in this country, both as a tree out of doors in warm climates, and as a tub plant in the North. Pruned to round, cone-shaped, or pyramid forms, bay trees are very popular tub plants both in Europe and America.

60

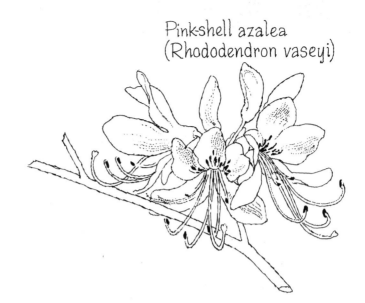

Pinkshell azalea
(Rhododendron vaseyi)

RHODODENRON

Rhododendrons belong to the same family (Ericaceae) as the mountain laurel. They are handsome shrubs or small trees, growing from seven to forty feet high. Most species have leathery evergreen leaves. Blooming in the spring, they are among the most beautiful of flowering shrubs. The large flowers are pink or yellow or purplish. Rhododendron, like laurel, is poisonous to eat.

They are found from Nova Scotia and New England west to Ohio, and south along the Allegheny Mountains to Georgia and Florida. One species, the pink-shell azalea (*Rhododendron vaseyi*) is on the threatened list in North Carolina. The Florida azalea (*Rhododendron austrinum*) is threatened in Georgia, Alabama, and Florida. Another species (*Rhododendron prunifolium*) is threatened in Alabama and Georgia.

61

ROSE MALLOW

The California rose mallow (*Hibiscus californicus*) belongs to the family Malvaceae. A lovely shrub, up to seven feet high, it grows only in California, in freshwater marshes and along river and lake banks. The beautiful white flowers have red centers. It is an endangered plant.

California rose mallow (Hibiscus californicus)

OAK

Oak trees (family Fagaceae) are tall, handsome ornamental trees with beautiful foliage. The bark of oak trees varies in color in different species. Some oaks have light gray or silvery gray bark;

others, dark gray or blackish; and still others, light brown, reddish brown, or dark brown. The flowers are in catkins or spikes. One-seeded nuts called acorns are the fruits. Acorns are eaten by wood rats and some other wild rats, and by mice, squirrels, raccoons, deer, and turkeys. Some Indians grind the nuts to make flour for mush or bread.

Most oaks are deciduous. This means that they shed their leaves in the fall of the year. But a few, which grow in warmer parts of the country, are evergreen. They keep their leaves all year round and are called live oaks.

Oak wood is valuable for lumber, and the bark is used for tanning leather.

There are more species of oak trees in the world than of any

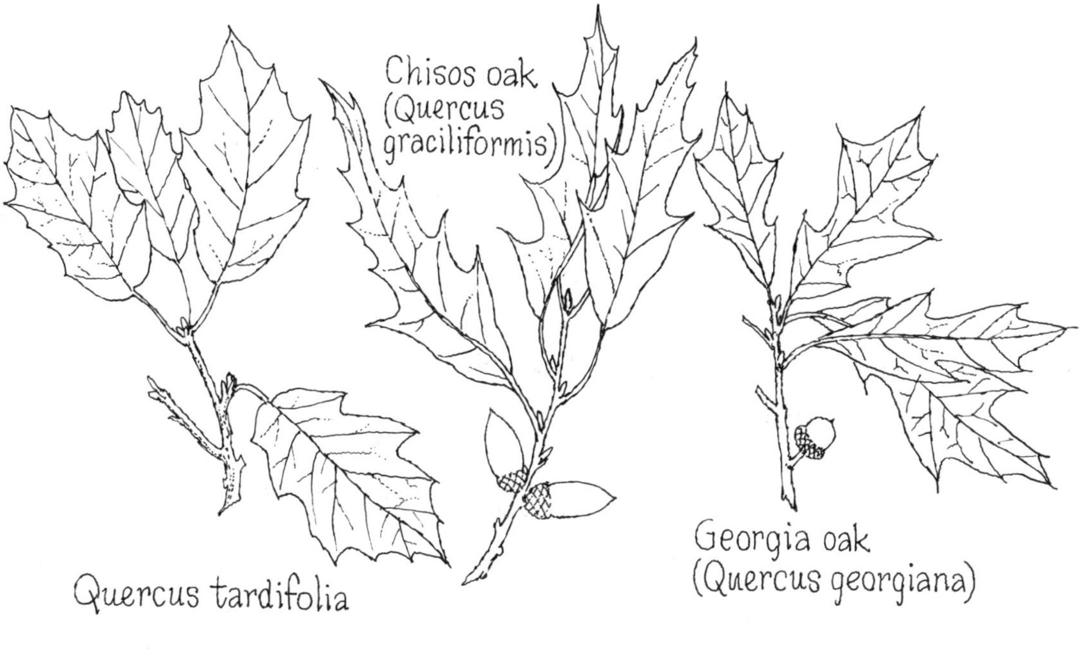

Chisos oak
(Quercus
graciliformis)

Georgia oak
(Quercus georgiana)

Quercus tardifolia

Island live oak
(Quercus tomentella)

other kind of trees. Over five hundred species exist, and of these about fifty species are native to the United States and Canada. You will see some kind of oak tree almost anywhere in the United States.

Three Texas oaks are endangered: *Quercus graciliformis*, *Quercus tardifolia*, and *Quercus hinckleyi*.

Five kinds of oak are on the threatened list: *Quercus georgiana* in South Carolina, Georgia, and Alabama; *Quercus oglethorpensis* in South Carolina and Georgia; *Quercus parvula* in California; *Quercus shumardii* var. *acerifolia* in Arkansas; and *Quercus tomentella* in California.

BREWER'S SPRUCE

Brewer's spruce (*Picea breweriana*) is the rarest of our native spruce trees. This handsome evergreen grows in a pyramid shape, from eighty to one hundred and twenty feet high, with branches often seven to eight feet long. The cones are purple.

Brewer's spruce is found mostly within five National Parks in the Siskiyou Mountains in southwestern Oregon and northwestern California where it is protected.

64

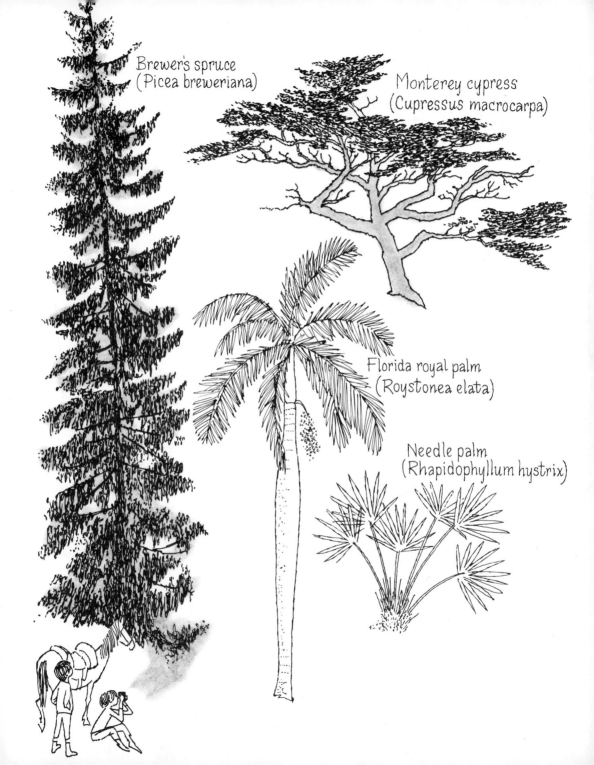

Brewer's spruce
(Picea breweriana)

Monterey cypress
(Cupressus macrocarpa)

Florida royal palm
(Roystonea elata)

Needle palm
(Rhapidophyllum hystrix)

FLORIDA ROYAL PALM

The Florida royal palm (*Roystonea elata*) is a magnificent tree that sometimes reaches one hundred and twenty-five feet in height. Far up the straight trunk is a cluster of long, feathery leaves. The leaves may reach fifteen feet in length. The golden-yellow flowers hang below the leaf clusters.

This palm is often planted along streets in towns and cities in southern Florida. It is protected in the Everglades National Park and in the Big Cypress Swamp, including Collier-Seminole State Park.

It is the only American palm that is endangered.

NEEDLE PALM, BLUE PALMETTO

This dwarf palm (*Rhapidophyllum hystrix*) is a beautiful little tree with an upright or creeping trunk of two to three feet in height. Sharp black spines, often a foot long, come from the fibers of the trunk. It grows only in the Deep South.

It is on the threatened list and on the list of trees collected too often by plant dealers in Alabama, Florida, Georgia, and Mississippi.

Certain rare trees are now protected within some National Forests and State Parks and Botanical Areas. It is against the law to cut timber for lumber in these areas.

66

CYPRESS

Among the rare trees found in western forests, mostly in California, are the ornamental cypress. They are evergreens with aromatic grayish-green foliage. Three native cypress are endangered or threatened. However, they are able to survive forest fires because the cones, when burned, open and drop the seeds on the ground, where they sprout.

The endangered Santa Cruz cypress (*Cupressus goveniana* var. *abramsiana*) appears in the Santa Cruz Mountains in central California.

The Cuyamaca cypress (*Cupressus arizonica* var. *stephensonii*) is a threatened tree found only in a single grove in the Cuyamaca Mountains in southern California. Protected in a one-mile stand of trees, it is partly in the Cleveland National Forest and partly within the Cuyamaca Rancho State Park.

The Piute cypress (*Cupressus arizonica* var. *nevadensis*) grows in the Piute Mountains in south central California. A threatened tree, it is now protected in nine groves in the Piute Cypress Botanical Area and the Sequoia National Forest.

TORREY PINE

Growing only in southern California, on the Pacific Coast, the Torrey pine (*Torreya californica*) is one of the rarest of the

Giant sequoia
(Sequoiadendron giganteum)

thirty-five pine species native to the United States. Most of the grove of seven thousand trees is protected within the Torrey Pine State Park.

GIANT SEQUOIA

The biggest, and one of the rarest, trees in America is the California big tree, the giant sequoia (*Sequoiadendron giganteum*). Found only in scattered groves in the Sierra Nevada Mountains in California, the sequoias grow from 250 to 280 feet high; a few reach 300 feet. The trunks are often twenty-four feet in diameter at a height of eight feet above the ground.

Sequoias are evergreens with cones from one to three inches long. They are among the oldest trees, and may live to be three thousand or more years old. Only the short, squat bristlecone pine (*Pinus aristata*) is said to be older.

The ancestors of both these trees were alive when dinosaurs roamed the earth, millions of years ago.

One of the sequoias in the Sequoia National Park, the General Sherman Tree, is the largest living thing in the world. It is 274.9 feet high, with a circumference of 102.6 feet at ground level, and 83.2 feet at four and a half feet above the ground. If the General Sherman Tree were harvested, it would yield 600,120 board feet of lumber, enough to build forty five-room houses.

The sequoias are given good protection in the Sequoia National Park and the Sequoia National Forest in California. It is now against the law to harvest the great trees growing within the park for lumber.

The first American tree to become extinct in the wild was named for Benjamin Franklin. The beautiful Franklin Tree (*Franklinia alatamaha*) can reach a height of thirty feet, and has fragrant white flowers, three inches across, with yellow stamens. In the fall of the year, its leaves turn bright red.

This tree was discovered by a Pennsylvania farmer, John Bartram, in the state of Georgia in 1765. By the year 1803 it was gone forever from the wilderness. It had been overcollected by plant dealers.

But you may still see a Franklin Tree today. Where? In the Bartram Gardens in Philadelphia, and in some other eastern gardens in this country where they have been grown from cuttings and seeds taken from Franklin Trees grown by Bartram in his aboretum. And three small specimens of these rare trees now grow in front of the National Museum of Natural History in Washington, D.C. You may also see them in Kew Gardens, in England.

Franklin Tree
(Franklinia alatamaha)

These rescued Franklin Trees stand as a reminder to us that we must conserve our native wild plants.

The government printed a picture of the Franklin Tree on a postage stamp in the year 1969.

A tree formerly believed to be extinct is the Ashe birch (*Betula uber*), a small birch with blackish bark which survives in the southern Appalachian Mountains. It was discovered by William Willard Ashe in 1914, in southwestern Virginia. Ashe was a forester of the United States Forest Service.

The Ashe birch was rediscovered in Virginia in 1975, after being "lost" for sixty years.

Do Not Pick

To return to common wild plants, the questions are often asked: "Which plants may I pick to put in a vase in my house? Which may I dig up in the wild to plant in pots, or in my own garden? Also, where may I go to get these plants?"

First, the DO NOT PICKs. You are not allowed to pick wild flowers in most public places including, as we have already said, the Wilderness and Primitive Areas in our National Forests. In other areas in our National Forests a special written permit is required to take out any plants.

Most state and local parks and nature centers do not allow you to pick or dig up plants. For example, in the state of Connecticut the Department of Environmental Protection says: "No person shall remove, destroy or otherwise injure any tree, flower, shrub, fern, moss . . ." in any state park or forest. You are asked instead to look, admire, and photograph.

Also, do not pick flowers along the roadside. In some areas, so many people are doing this that certain roadside plants are in danger.

What You May Pick

Then, where could you pick a bouquet of wild flowers? In your own backyard. If you live on a farm, pick in your own field or woods. If you have a friend who owns a farm, get his permission to pick on his farm. If you live on a ranch, pick there. Or, if you have a friend who lives on a ranch, get his permission.

Now, what flowers should you pick? We repeat—do not even touch any of the plants on the endangered or threatened lists. Pick only very, very common flowers.

You might, for example, pick a bunch of wild daisies. By this we mean the oxeye daisy (*Chrysanthemum leucanthemum*), the common daisy of field and pasture throughout most of the United

States. This is the daisy to gather to make a daisy chain. It has a pretty white flower with a yellow center, blossoming on stems from fifteen to twenty-five inches high. Since it grows like a weed, farmers often call it white-weed.

The oxeye daisy is not, however, a native plant. Its ancestors came here from Europe and Asia. It now is so common in our country that it is not in danger of being overpicked.

When cutting flowers, use scissors or shears so as not to disturb the roots, as you may when you pull stems by hand.

To Dig Up and Pot

Suppose that you want to dig up a wild flower to put in a clay pot. Once again, be sure to choose a common plant, one that is not endangered or threatened.

Remember, you are not allowed to dig up wild flowers in most public places. And, of course, do not dig up wild flowers along roadsides.

But if you are going to dig up a wild plant on your own land, or have permission to dig on a neighbor's land, a good choice would be yarrow (*Achillea millefolium*).

Like the oxeye daisy, yarrow came here from Europe. The common yarrow is found in pastures and meadows throughout most of the United States. It is a perennial plant, with stems from one to two feet high. The flowers are white. It blossoms during the summer months.

To dig up a yarrow plant, first pull away weeds and trash around the plant. Use a sharp trowel. Take a good clump of soil, so as not to disturb the roots. Choose a clay pot to plant it in, and spread a few pieces of broken clay pot or pebbles over the hole in the bottom. This lets water drain out without getting stale. Settle the plant gently in the pot with the bottom of the stem about a half inch below the top of the pot. Add more soil around the roots if necessary.

Set the pot on the porch in summer. In winter, set the pot on a sunny window sill. The plant must get sun at least half of the day. And water it, at least once a day, twice if the soil dries out.

For Growing in Your Garden

One of the commonest weeds of lawns and gardens in the United States is the dandelion (*Taraxacum officinale*). It, too, like the oxeye daisy and yarrow, is an immigrant from Europe and Asia.

The pretty golden-yellow flowers grow on hollow, milky-juiced stalks from two to eighteen inches high. The flower heads are from one to two inches across. The green leaves are toothed and come not from the stalks, but from the top of the deep, thick root. The seeds ripen into a silky-haired globe.

Dandelion leaves can be used as "greens" and cooked like

spinach. So, dig up the weedy dandelions that appear, unwanted, in your lawn and among the flowers and vegetables in your garden. Put them in a row, about a foot apart, in a sunny spot in your garden. In this way you can raise a green vegetable without buying seeds.

And of course cut off the flowers of your garden dandelions before they go to seed, to prevent them from spreading.

How to Enjoy Endangered Plants

We wish to stress that the best way to enjoy rare wild plants, from flowers to trees, is to look at them in the wild where they grow naturally. Walk along a country roadside. Hike in the mountains and down into the valleys and out onto the plains. If you live near a desert, hike there. See what species are growing on a river bank or by a pond or in the water.

Enjoy the beautiful, rare native plants in their own homeland. That is the place where they grow best and live longest. If you would like to enjoy them in your own home, we repeat, do not transplant them into a pot or your own garden, but photograph them. And hang their pictures on your walls.

In this way you will be helping to save beautiful, rare plants now on the endangered or threatened or commercially exploited lists from becoming extinct.

Appendix 1

The Smithsonian Institution List

REPORT ON ENDANGERED AND THREATENED PLANT SPECIES OF THE UNITED STATES PRESENTED TO THE CONGRESS OF THE UNITED STATES OF AMERICA BY THE SECRETARY, SMITHSONIAN INSTITUTION.

This includes:

Recommendations for Preservation of Endangered Species of Plants.

List of Commercially Exploited Species in the Continental United States.

List of Recently Extinct and Possibly Extinct Species of Higher Plants in the Continental United States (100).

List of Endangered Species in the Continental United States (761).

List of Threatened Species in the Continental United States (1,238).

State Lists of Endangered and Threatened Species in the Continental United States.

List of Endangered and Threatened, and Recently Extinct, Species of Hawaii.

See also E. S. Ayensu and R. A. DeFilipps, *Endangered and Threatened Plants of the United States.* Smithsonian Institution and Wildlife Fund, Inc. (1977).

Among the best places to get your questions on endangered local plants answered is the department of botany at your state university, or a botanical garden near you. There are also many regional societies such as The New England Wildflower Society, Framingham, Massachusetts; The California Native Plant Society, Davis, California; and the Georgia Conservatory, Atlanta, Georgia.

Appendix 2

Cactus Dealers Who Raise Their Plants from Seeds

Cactus by Mueller, 10411 Rosedale Highway, Bakersfield, California 93308. Catalog.

California Cactus Nursery, 19721 Krameria Avenue, Perris, California 92370. Cactus seedlings, wholesale only.

Desert Hill Cactus Growers, Box 123, Corona, California 91720. Mail order only. Send stamped, self-addressed envelope for plant list.

Grotes Cactus Gardens, 13555 South Leland Road, Oregon City, Oregon 97045. Twenty-five cents for catalog.

Henrietta's Nursery, 1345 North Brawley Avenue, Fresno, California 93705. Thirty-five cents for catalog.

Modlin's Cactus Gardens, 2416 El Corto, Vista, California 92083. Twenty-five cents for catalog.

Appendix 3

Conservation Associations

Among the many botanical gardens and research centers that have experts on their staffs, publish conservation booklets, and also publish magazines are:

The American Fern Society, New York Chapter, the New York Botanical Garden, Bronx, New York 10458.
American Fern Journal, published quarterly.
Fiddlehead Forum, newsletter, published bimonthly.
American Forestry Association, 1319 18 Street N.W., Washington, D.C. 20036.
American Forests, published monthly.
The Brooklyn Botanic Garden, Brooklyn, New York 11225.
Plants and Gardens, published quarterly.
The Connecticut Agricultural Experiment Station, New Haven, Connecticut 06504.
Frontiers of Plant Science, published in May and November.
National Parks and Conservation Association, 1701 18 Street N.W., Washington, D.C. 20009.
National Parks and Conservation Magazine: The Environmental Journal, published monthly.
The Nature Conservancy, 1800 North Kent Street, Arlington, Virginia 22209.
The Nature Conservancy News, published quarterly.
The New York Botanical Garden, Bronx, New York 10458.
Garden, published bimonthly.
Science Service, 1719 N Street N.W., Washington D.C. 20036.
Science News, published weekly.
Smithsonian Association, 900 Jefferson Drive, Washington, D.C. 20560.
Smithsonian, published monthly.

Index

80

Dorothy Childs Hogner is a Connecticut Yankee born in Manhattan. The daughter of a doctor, she lived the first year of her life in New York. Then her family moved to an old white clapboard house on a hundred-acre farm in Connecticut.

Mrs. Hogner attended Wellesley College in Massachusetts, Parsons School of Design in New York, and was graduated from the University of New Mexico. She is the author of many books for children, nearly all of which were illustrated by her late husband, Nils Hogner. She has also written adult books—three on the growing and use of herbs, and three travel books. Mrs. Hogner lives on an herb farm in Litchfield, Connecticut.

Arabelle Wheatley is the illustrator of more than a dozen books for children, on subjects that range from mosquitoes to beachcombing. Her interest in plants and animals began when she was a child exploring her grandfather's farm near Wind Ridge, Pennsylvania. Mrs. Wheatley studied at the Art Institute of Pittsburgh and then worked in New York, in advertising and book publishing, for several years. Now she and her husband spend their winters in Arcadia, Florida, and their summers near Wind Ridge, where they have restored an old house on a hundred acres of rugged hill country.